Economic$ in Colorado

Joe Rhatigan

Table of Contents

Chapter 1: Economic Incentives in Colorado . 4

Chapter 2: Colorado's Economy 16

Chapter 3: Personal Financial Literacy 24

Chapter 4: Fannie Mae Duncan:
Entrepreneur Extraordinaire 34

Glossary 38

Index 39

Economics in Your Community 40

Economic Incentives in Colorado

Your teacher assigns you homework. Why do you do it? If you do, you might earn a good grade. If you don't do it, your grade might drop. A good grade is an **incentive**. It is a reward. Getting a low grade is a **disincentive**.

An economy has incentives and disincentives too. The economy is the part of society that has to do with making and spending money. People spend their money on goods and services. Goods are products people want that they can buy. For example, apples and cars are goods. Services are things people do for each other, such as cutting hair or providing childcare. Incentives make people want to spend their money.

Inside and Out

What makes you want to do things? Some incentives come from inside you, like wanting to have fun. Some come from outside you, like a grown-up in your life telling you what to do.

Have you seen people get excited about a sale? A sale is when you can buy something for less than normal. Why would a store do this? Sales are incentives for their customers. When things cost less, people buy more. They might even spend more money overall on other things once they go to the store for the sale.

There are many kinds of incentives for people to buy and sell. Sometimes, the government makes the incentive. For instance, people might get a **tax** break when they buy certain things. This means they pay lower taxes. Sometimes, conditions are an incentive. For example, many people like carrots. The fact that there are many customers who want carrots makes farmers want to plant them. Sellers want to give people what they want to buy.

Copycats

Sometimes, an item for sale becomes very popular. People buy it fast. Other sellers see this success. They may make imitations to sell themselves. This is why once something becomes popular, you may start to see many copycats of it.

Natural resources can also be an incentive. People can sell them to make money. They can also use them to make other things that can be sold. Businesses have an incentive to make things from resources that are easy to get. For example, if a builder needs wood, they might open a business near a forest.

Coal is one of Colorado's major resources. It is mined and sold. It has always been a resource. But it has not always been in high **demand**. Today, coal is used to make energy. The demand for it around the world is high. So, there is also high incentive for coal to be mined and sold.

However, burning coal can also pollute the air. For that reason, some people want to make energy in another way. Wind is one way. There is now an incentive to build wind turbines. The turbines make energy without pollution.

a power plant in Boulder

Long-Term Thinking

Climate change is one reason to be **eco-friendly**. But there can be an incentive to make money now rather than care for the planet's health. This is thinking in the short-term (for right now) rather than the long-term (for the future).

The Fur Trade

Today, we have fabrics for warmth. But long ago, people used animal furs. They were in high demand. This created an incentive for fur trapping.

In Colorado, the Ute and Puebloan peoples traded furs. They did this long before people from Europe came. Later, European settlers traded glass and metal for these furs. They sold the furs in Europe. The furs became very popular. This created an incentive too.

Soon, the people of Europe wanted more. They wanted beaver furs. So, traders hunted more beavers. Then, they wanted bison furs. Traders hunted more bison. Over time, there were fewer animals left to hunt. The demand was higher than the resource. Some animals nearly went extinct. This can happen when a resource is overused.

beaver furs

Bison Today

By 1884, there were only 325 bison left. There once were millions! In the 1900s, people worked hard to save them. Today, there are thousands.

A Golden Opportunity

In the late 1850s, there were rumors of gold in the West. Some of the gold was in Colorado. Before then, few settlers from Europe traveled here. There was no reason for them to. It was hard to get here. It was unknown to them too. Most of the people who called it home were American Indians. They had lived in the area for a long time.

Central City in the 1800s

In 1857, people in the East had economic problems. Gold was an incentive for them to go west. Many did. This caused the Colorado gold rush of 1859. The gold rush and **influx** of people, in turn, led to Colorado becoming a territory and later a state. This expanded the United States. It also forced many American Indians from their land.

Nightingale Gold Mine at Bull Hill

Fifty-Niners

Have you heard of Forty-Niners? They were miners from the California gold rush of 1849. Miners from the Colorado gold rush were called Fifty-Niners.

Nature's Incentive

Farming is important in Colorado, especially in the eastern part of the state. The land there is flat, and the climate is dry. In the past, farmers dug ditches to change the flow of rivers and bring water to their land. When droughts came, their crops died and they lost money. This was a disincentive to farm.

Farmers today have incentive to use new methods. Some use **dryland farming**. They only use water that falls from the sky, and they do not reroute rivers and streams. They also plant **cover crops** to keep water in the soil when fields are not in use. In these ways, they work with the climate they have. There is much less chance of the crops and land being destroyed.

This field of alfalfa is a cover crop.

The Dust Bowl

In the 1900s, farmers in the Great Plains dug up all the grasses and replaced them with the crops they wanted. This ruined the natural cycles of the growth in the land. When drought came, the land turned to dust and created enormous dust storms. This caused the Dust Bowl of the 1930s.

Chapter 2

Colorado's Economy

Do you shop for your food? Buy your clothes? Go to the movies? Have you ever sold cookies or candy to support your school or team? Does your family pay rent or a **mortgage** to live in your home? If so, you are part of the economy.

Every place has its own economy. The economy in Colorado has changed over time. Some industries have become less important. Others have become more so. Some have always been important. People here, like everywhere, turn resources into goods and services. It takes hard work to do this. So, workers are a necessary part of the economy.

Unions

A **labor union** is a group of workers who join together. They do this to protect each other. Sometimes, companies try to cut costs. They might do this by treating their workers poorly. Unions talk to the company or go on **strike** to make sure their needs are met.

Natural Resources

Colorado's natural resources include minerals, coal, farmland, wind, and more. All of these can be used to create goods and services. Long ago, the Ute Indian Tribe used many of these same resources. They used animals for food. They used plants for food and medicine. They traded for pottery and more.

The settlers from Europe used some of these resources differently. The Ute people moved from hunting ground to hunting ground. They did this so they would not overuse one place by taking too much from it. The settlers, on the other hand, wanted to do just what their name says: settle. They wanted to put down roots. They built towns and farms. To do this, they forced the Ute people and others living there from the land.

snow-capped Rockies across a valley

A Ute artist is painting traditional designs on a modern pot.

The Ute Indian Tribe Today

The Ute Indian Tribe has always lived in Colorado. Today, there are three official tribes: the Southern Ute Indian Tribe, the Ute Mountain Ute Tribe, and the Northern Ute Tribe in Utah.

Tourism

Colorado's natural resources help shape its economy. Gold led to mining. Grasslands led to farming. Wild game led to the fur trade. One key resource is Colorado's natural beauty. This led to tourism.

The Rocky Mountains pass through the state. There are 58 mountains here that are taller than 14,000 feet (4,267 meters). To the west, there are colorful mesas. Mesas are mountains with flat tops. The Grand Mesa is among them. It is the largest mesa in the world.

People flock to climb these mountains. They visit the national parks and are awed by the views. They stay at hotels and campgrounds. They eat at restaurants. They spend their money all over the state. This makes tourism a leading industry.

Grand Mesa is one of Colorado's most famous landmarks.

Human Resources

People can be a resource too. In Colorado, skiing is an important industry. Ski towns need workers who come just for the winter. Without those workers, the industry would suffer.

Energy

Coal mining in Colorado began in the 1800s. Coal can be burned to make energy. After the gold rush, many gold miners became coal miners. But coal mining was (and is) dangerous work. It was unhealthy to breathe the air in a mine. There were also cave-ins and explosions. Workers formed unions. They went on strike for more money and safer ways to work.

Coal mining is still a leading industry. But Colorado makes energy in other ways too. One of these is wind power. In fact, the state is a leader in the use of wind power. There are government incentives for people to use it. Why? Because it is good for the environment and creates new jobs.

The Ludlow strike of 1913–14 is famous for changing worker conditions.

Supply and Demand

When there is a big **supply** of something, it may sell for a low price. People will not pay too much for it because they can get it easily somewhere else. But if the supply is low and the demand is high, sellers can ask higher prices. People will pay the high price just to get the item.

Chapter 3

Personal Financial Literacy

When it comes to money, goods, and services, there are many choices to make. There is a limited amount of money and resources. Each person decides how to spend their money. Each business or government also decides how to use its resources.

When there are choices, that means there are **alternatives**. But keep in mind that most choices come with a loss. The loss is the alternative you did not choose. This is also called the **opportunity cost**. It is what we give up when we choose something else. If you have five dollars to spend, you could choose to buy candy now. Or, you could save it to spend later on something that costs more. Let's say you decide to save up for a toy. The candy is your opportunity cost.

DEDUC

Employees NI

x

90.00

10.05

Work Hard, Earn More?

Some people do not earn much money no matter how hard they work. Their **income** is low, even when they work long hours. This is often because their **wages** are low. Other people may also work hard but earn a much higher income. Their wages are high.

Life is filled with choices. Have you ever chosen to buy something small now instead of saving for later? Do you see the adults in your life choosing how to spend their money? Everyone has to make choices when it comes to cost.

But sometimes, an opportunity cost is not about money. If you choose to play soccer instead of being in the school play, the cost is the fun you might have had in the play. If you choose to play video games instead of doing your homework, the cost may be your good grades. Often, when we make a choice, we decide the cost is worth it. But sometimes, we choose to ignore the cost. Then, we might make a not-so-good decision. The cost always comes due.

Pros and Cons

How do you make decisions? One way is to make a list of pros (good things) and cons (bad things). A pros and cons list can help you think logically!

Pros:

Cons:

People through time have had to think about opportunity costs. Farmers decide what kinds of crops to grow and how to grow them. They think about the future too. Is the crop right for the land? Will they make money after all their hard work?

Families must decide on opportunity costs as well. A place to live is often one of the biggest expenses people have. Should they buy their home and **maintain** it themselves? Maintenance is part of the cost of owning something. Should they rent their home? Then, a landlord is responsible to maintain it, but the landlord makes decisions about their home too. Should they live with other family or friends? They can share expenses, but they have to share space as well.

Sometimes, the only choice people have is what they can afford. People think about what they can afford and opportunity costs when they make decisions about spending.

Investment

If you put money into a business or opportunity, this is an **investment**. For example, a farmer can invest in new equipment. A person can invest in certain companies to own a piece of them. The person then shares in the **profits**.

A government must make choices too. For example, Colorado has created many parks to protect its wilderness. This means the state can't sell the park resources. People can't mine or sell the land. Colorado has decided that this choice is worth it. The land and wildlife are protected. At the same time, the state has let go of the opportunity to make a lot of money right now. Why? It is an investment in the future.

People who make decisions like these may not even be the ones to benefit from them. The payoff may go to people yet to come. A tree planted today may only become fully grown long after the planter is gone. The choice is not for now. It is the right thing to do for tomorrow.

Garden of the Gods near Colorado Springs

Rocky Mountain National Park

This amazing place became a national park in 1915. It is one of the most visited spots in the United States. People come from all over to see its mountains, lakes, and wildlife.

Cashing in on Colorado

Colorado has mining. It has energy. It has tourism. It has farming. And it has so much more! In fact, its economy is filled with opportunities. When it comes to goods, services, and money, there are plenty of choices to be made.

The resources and history of the state play key roles in its economy. You can't have Rocky Mountain National Park without the Rocky Mountains. Colorado wouldn't be the state it is today without all the people who have lived and worked there.

The economy is important in Colorado. It is important in your own life too. It is good to think hard about the choices you make, just as Colorado's leaders must do. You can make choices that are good for you, and good for Colorado too!

A park ranger talks to tourists and answers their questions.

Jobs of the Future

Thousands of people in Colorado have jobs making renewable energy. More jobs are being created in this industry every day!

Fannie Mae Duncan: Entrepreneur Extraordinaire

Fannie Mae Duncan was born in 1918. When she was fifteen, her family moved to Colorado Springs. She went to an **integrated** school there. This type of school was rare in those days.

Duncan was African American. Laws and customs of the time forced people of different races to live, eat, and work apart. Black people didn't have the same rights as white people. Duncan knew this was wrong. She knew that all people should be treated equally.

Duncan wanted a chance to succeed. She found it through hard work and leaping at opportunities. First, she managed a soda counter. Next, she opened her own cafe. She became a big success. Soon, she owned a barbershop too. Then, she bought a beauty parlor, a record store, and more!

What's an Entrepreneur?

An entrepreneur is someone who starts a business. Starting a business takes a lot of money. It can be risky. It takes hard work and plenty of time. But it can really pay off.

Workers pose at Duncan's Cafe, one of Duncan's many businesses.

Duncan is most famous for the Cotton Club. It was a night club with music and dancing. Most clubs for white people didn't allow Black musicians to play. But some of the most popular musicians were Black, such as Louis Armstrong and Billie Holiday. Duncan invited them to her club. She also invited people of all races to see them perform.

She hired people of different races to run the club as well. This angered many white people. The police chief asked her to keep white people out. But Duncan put a sign in her window. It said, "Everybody Welcome." This was her mission. Now, it is her legacy too.

Louis Armstrong and Billie Holiday were popular artists.

New York Namesake

Duncan named her club after a popular club in New York. That club also hired Black performers. But it only allowed white people in the audience. Duncan's club welcomed everyone.

Glossary

alternatives—options, choices

cover crops—crops that protect and enrich soil

demand—how much of something people want

disincentive—something that may cause a person to not do something

dryland farming—growing plants for food using only the water that falls from the sky as rain

eco-friendly—not harmful to the environment

incentive—something that makes someone work hard

income—the amount of money a person earns on a regular basis, through work, investments, or profits

influx—the arrival of a large number of people or large amount of something

integrated—with all people participating, often referring to Black and white people together

investment—the process of spending money in order to profit

labor union—a group of workers who come together to protect their working rights and pay

maintain—to keep something in good shape

mortgage—a legal contract in which a person borrows a large amount of money to buy property and pays it back over time

natural resources—materials that come from nature and can be used to make money

opportunity cost—the value of what is given up when making a choice

profits—money made after expenses are paid

strike—the stopping of work in an attempt to force an employer to agree to demands

supply—how much of something is available

tax—money collected by a government from its citizens to pay for schools, roads, and more

wages—money earned by working a job

Index

choice(s), 24, 26, 28, 30, 32

coal, 8, 18, 22

Cotton Club, 36

disincentive(s), 4, 14

dryland farming, 14

Duncan, Fannie Mae, 34–37

Dust Bowl, 15

entrepreneurs, 34–35

European settlers, 10, 12, 18

farming, 14, 20, 32

Fifty–Niners, 13

fur trade, 10, 20

gold rush, 12–13, 22

Great Plains, 15

incentive(s), 4–6, 8–10, 13–14, 22

income, 25

investment, 29–30

labor union, 17

mesas, 20

natural resources, 8, 18, 20

opportunity cost(s), 24, 26, 28

Puebloan peoples, 10

renewable energy, 33

Rocky Mountain National Park, 31–32

Rocky Mountains, 20, 32

tourism, 20, 32

Ute Indian Tribe, 18–19

wages, 25

wind energy, 8, 18, 22

Economics in Your Community

Each country, state, city, and community has its own economy. This economy may change over time. What can you tell about your community's economy just by looking around? What stores have closed or what businesses have opened? Research this economy online or by talking with people about the work they do.

Once you have a good idea as to how people around you make money, think about a business you could start. Here are some things to think about:

1. Why do you think this business will succeed?

2. What resources will you need?

3. Who would want to buy your goods and services?

4. What will you charge for your goods or services?

As an extra challenge, design an advertisement for your business!